Trek to the Manger

Advent Devotions for Women on the Move

Brita Hammit

Cover Art: Narongsak Yaisumlee/Shutterstock.com

ISBN-10: 0692305858

ISBN-13: 978-0692305850 (Pink Shoes Ministries)

IN MEMORY OF

Mrs. Waring - the Sunday School teacher who gave me my first blank book with the invitation to make it my own.

Clareen Barrett - who taught me that every day is a blank canvas to God - and He doesn't skimp on the paint.

CONTENTS

Welcome to Trek to the Manger   i

1   Preparing for Advent: A Trek to the Manger   1

2   Orientation for the Journey   3

3   If You Were Stranded on a Deserted Island...   7

4   Saddle Up Your Camel   12

5   Traveling Buddies   16

6   Passport, Please   21

7   They Say It's Your Birthday   25

8   Spiritual Self Defense   29

9   (Almost) Derailed   34

10   Window Washing   38

11   Space Cadets   43

12   Sprinkles   47

13   A New Generation of Trekkies   51

14   Holy GPS!   55

15   (Spiritually) Homeless   59

16   Tend to Your Knitting   64

17   Purposeful Acts of Kindness   68

18   9 1/2 Miles Per Hour   72

19   99 Bottles of Beer on the Wall   78

20   Kingdom Business 101   84

21   Gift Selection Day   88

22   Tour Guides   93

23   Turn! Turn! Turn!   98

24   Stinky Friday   103

25   I Call Shotgun!   107

26   Road Closed   111

27   Are We There Yet?   116

28   Aglow   120

29   Unveiled (Driving With the Top Down)   126

WELCOME TO
TREK TO THE MANGER

In these pages you will find daily thoughts and challenges for the season of Advent, which begins on the fourth Sunday before Christmas and ends with the celebration of Christ's birth on Christmas Eve.

To coordinate your journey with others on the Trek, visit <u>pinkshoesministries.me</u> and click on *Trek to the Manger*.

May your faith walk (or run!) be *inspired* and your heart *set on fire* as the Spirit of God sets your feet onto this narrow road.

This road that ends nowhere short of the coming of Emmanuel.

This **Trek to the Manger**.

1 PREPARING FOR ADVENT: A TREK TO THE MANGER

I honestly begin to dread the coming holiday season about now…

Too much food.
Too much on the calendar.
Too much on the credit card bill.

And not enough joy.

If you're anything like me, you already know full well what your personal challenges and struggles with the holidays are, but do you know that *this year can be different*?

During this season of Advent, join me daily for a Trek to the Manger.

Not only can we find ways to focus on Christ in the midst of too much of *everything,* but I believe we can also find ways to make the trek through this season a thing of JOY for ourselves and for those who share our world.

Traveling is not without its challenges, however,

and any trek we make will be easier if we can find ways to lighten our load.

So, I have to ask you...

What is weighing you down as the holiday season approaches?

Has anything been bugging you for so long that you're nearly desperate to just deal with it and move on?

What areas of your life need to be weeded out, sifted through, retooled, or redefined?

Take time today to wrestle with these questions, in preparation for the journey ahead. Ask God to use this season of anticipation to prepare you for the answers you seek!

Together, let's take hold of this predictably chaotic season for the *glory* of the Savior we celebrate!

(Better dig those trail shoes out of the closet - you're going to need them as our adventure begins!)

2 ORIENTATION FOR THE JOURNEY

Have you ever wondered what the journey was like for the Wise Men - that storied trio whose travels brought them to meet the Messiah? Somehow they managed to arrive at their destination, guided by a single star in the sky.

They must have been so focused on the light!

The beginning of the season of Advent marks a unique opportunity for believers to start moving, as the Wise Men did, toward the Light of the World.

What if we could experience some of what the Wise Men of old must have felt as they began journeying toward the star?

Anticipation. Excitement. Curiosity. Wonder.

When was the last time *you* felt that way about the holiday season we're about to enter?

We, like the Wise Men, have gifts to bring to the Christ child.

We may not know what those gifts are (yet), but

discovering them is part of the journey.

We, like the Wise Men, must also be willing to deliver those gifts to Him. As one who rarely succeeds at packing light, I'm aware of the implications of baggage. Lightening our load so we can handle Jesus' gift is also part of the journey.

It's no wonder that the enemy of God loves the holiday season! Not because it ends at the manger, in celebration of the coming of God in human flesh, but because there are so many opportunities for believers to be distracted from what this season is *really* about.

During Advent, on our Trek to the Manger, we are going to deal with the contents of our baggage and the way we move through this journey in both *practical* and *deeply spiritual* ways.

But the last thing we need this Advent season is more to *do*, so I won't be laying anything heavy on you. This Trek is designed to help you *lift* the burdens you carry and *lighten* your load...

Emotionally. Relationally. Practically. Spiritually.

We'll be doing this together, using:

Star Sightings
Each daily Trek will provide suggestions for keeping our focus on the Light of the World – *on Jesus*. Watching for His light each day will give us direction during this season of choices, filled with attractive paths *everywhere;* making a straight shot to the manger difficult to find.

Daily Giveaways
The Daily Giveaway is a challenge to lighten your load and keep you footloose on the journey. By participating in the Daily Giveaway, you will have an opportunity to develop the habit of staying free of the stuff of this world by choosing to live generously. Your Daily Giveaway isn't something *I give to you,* but something *you give away.*

Journal the Journey
While you're at it, why not keep a travelogue – a journal of your responses, thoughts, and actions - while participating in the Trek? *Record the challenges* you make to yourself. *Track the joy* you are going to feel and create!

Join the Conversation
You are not on this journey alone!

I don't know about you, but I often hear God speak through the struggles, questions, and insights of those I travel through life with. Take time on the Trek to share your thoughts with fellow sojourners; consider Trekking with a family member, your small group or even a distant friend. *Traveling is so much richer when the adventure is shared!*

Before beginning our journey we've got to strap on a pair of sturdy shoes to insure we will be able to traverse any terrain we may encounter; through any conditions we find ourselves in along the way.

Prayer is the act of tying our spiritual shoes. Before we set out on this shared adventure, will you join me in tying a tight triple-knot in those laces?

God of the Journey, we hear Your call and long to see the Light of Your Presence in this world during the weeks ahead. We know we will need Your constant touch in order to be alert to all that You are doing around us, so we ask You to send Your Holy Spirit to our hearts.

Make room inside us for the new birth You want to see in our lives; not just in the distant future, but in the Advent weeks ahead. Bring to life the risen Jesus in our ordinary human bodies, just as You placed Your own life into Jesus' human body here on earth.

We don't know what You're going to do with our Trek to the Manger, but we know You'll do something beautiful, so... we wait. And we watch.
Come, Lord Jesus.
Amen.

3 *IF YOU WERE STRANDED ON A DESERTED ISLAND...*

We begin our Trek in the vein of the age-old question:

If you were stranded on a deserted island and could take only three things, what would those things be?

I'm willing to bet it wouldn't take long for you to decide on your three. Doesn't it seem completely ridiculous, in light of the quantity of possessions we store in boxes, closets, garages, and attics, that what we really *need* is so much less than what we already *have*?

Our attempt to follow the path of the Wise Men prompts a good hard look at what we carry around. Personally, I can't make a trip to the store without my ten-pound purse, stocked with more than I could possibly need for every conceivable situation – *ever*. In addition to the chronic neck and shoulder pain my handbag creates, I could easily be the poster child for an even weightier problem:

The tendency to accumulate more than we

choose to give away.

One response to the problem might be to simply pack a box with our excess possessions and drop it off at the local thrift store, but I'd like to propose an even better way:

"At this time you have plenty. What you have can help others who are in need. Then later, when they have plenty, they can help you when you are in need, and all will be equal. As it is written in the Scriptures, 'The person who gathered more did not have too much, nor did the person who gathered less have too little.'"
2 Corinthians 8:14-15 *(NCV)*

When we as believers, followers of the Light of the World, find ourselves in possession of plenty, we can be sure that there are others who are in need of the overflow.

Star Sighting
We receive strength, energy, and momentum for the journey from the life-giving Spirit of God alive within us. Similarly, our life-breath can be literally sucked right out of us by those things which weigh us down, rob us of our joy, and leach away our energy.

Take inventory of the things in your life that shine light, bring joy, elicit smiles, and create energy. In all likelihood, this list is where you'll catch your first glimpse of the Star – the Light of the World – on your Trek to the Manger.

1 John 1:5 tells us:

"God is light; in him there is no darkness at all."
(NIV)

That which illuminates our lives is often steeped in God-presence.

Pay attention to the sources of light in your day and add *that* to your baggage! Darkness results in overweight bags every time, but Light is by its nature... *light.*

Daily Giveaway

Rather than a blind donation, which serves mostly to make you feel better, take time to consider your abundance today. What do you own *in excess* that could be given away to a particular person or family to help meet a *need* and to create *joy* in the process?

My church family has a clothing exchange event twice each year. At a recent exchange I picked up an adorable vest from a table piled with donations – faux fur, leopard print – very fun! One of the teenagers from church also liked the vest, but I ended up taking it home. Sometime later, the vest resurfaced in my jam-packed closet and I realized that the joy this young lady would feel to receive the vest trumped the fun of wearing it myself, so I gave it away. The resulting bear hug and toothy grin were well worth the sacrifice.

Usually our gift giving during the holiday season is done over the course of a few hours on Christmas morning, or if we're lucky, over a few days spent with family and friends.

What if we decided not to limit our generosity to those who will sit around the tree with us this year?

Instead, what if we were to use the season of Advent to develop a *habit* of giving - one that marks our *lives*, not just our holidays?

Issued with each Trek devotion is an invitation for you to give something away. Today, why not take a look in your closet...

Do you see anything your daughter has been coveting that she would be surprised to receive as a gift?

Is there something hanging there that your sister or best friend might love to wear?

Which item makes you think fondly of someone else? What if you were to give that item to her, with that sentiment?

Don't wait for Christmas! Give it away - today!

For this day, don't worry about the things that weigh you down. For this day, look *only* for the *Light*.

Tomorrow will take care of itself.

4 SADDLE UP YOUR CAMEL

With just a few precious possessions loaded into our travel packs, today is the day we saddle up the camel and begin to move toward the manger!

Star Sighting
For the Wise Men, the journey began with the light of a new star in the sky – a star they somehow knew was connected to the birth of the King.

Doesn't this make you ask questions? Don't you wonder what prompted them to make the journey? How did they know about the star in the first place? What made them think they would actually, finally, *arrive* at the location heralded by the light?

Many of us are in a holding pattern today. We're feeling the need to *move on, move out,* or *move forward*, but we're waiting. We're waiting for God to give us a sign. We want a star to follow, too!

If we're completely honest, we don't *just* want a sign, but a map and an itinerary as well. We want to know what comes next, each step of the way, *before* we set out. We don't want to enter the risky unknown; we want confirmation that we're on the right path at *every* point along the route!

The disconcerting truth is that God promises to guide us on the journey; not to map it out for us in advance. He set a star in the sky for the Wise Men to follow. He set a cloud by day and a pillar of fire by night for the Israelites to follow. And in Jesus' own words, as recorded in Matthew 10:38, God instructs us to *"Take up your cross and follow me."*

No map. No itinerary. And a cross to carry on our backs.

Waiting as we do for *God's will for my life* only serves to keep us from starting the journey at all.

Remember the Israelites, as they were about to enter the land God had promised? God instructed them to cross the Jordan River and enter the Promised Land, but there was one serious problem: the Jordan was at flood stage. It wasn't safe to cross.

In a seemingly counterintuitive move, God instructed the priests to step into the water *first*; only *then* would He stop the river's flow so the people could cross in safety (Joshua chapter 3).

God didn't make a way for Israel until Israel began to make their way.

Some of what needs to happen in our lives isn't going to happen until we saddle up our camels and get our feet wet in the rivers of life.

Today, let's ask God to help us fix our eyes on this truth. With Jesus ahead of us on the path, we begin this Advent journey. Following Him, we will arrive at the right time, in the right place.

Just as the Wise Men did.

Daily Giveaway
Not everything that hinders our journey is a material thing. In fact, if you're anything like me, you get in your *own* way more often than not.

Waiting on God's will for my life often translates into doing things *my way* in the meantime. As a result, I create control issues that hold me captive within the confines of my comfort zone, keeping me from traversing the risky road of faith.

Ask yourself today:

What am I holding onto that keeps me from getting my feet wet with God?

What am I waiting on God for?

What keeps me from moving forward in my walk with Him?

Today we choose to give away our need to know the entire plan before shouldering our crosses and following our Lord! After all, if the Wise Men had demanded every detail up front, would they have even *started* their Trek to the Manger?

Journal the Journey
Take time today to download your thoughts into your travelogue. Maybe even share them for others to connect with and learn from.

Then get your feet wet!

What do we have to lose?

5 *TRAVELING BUDDIES*

As far as we know, three Wise Men began a journey to follow the star, and the *same* three Wise Men completed that journey… together.

As far as we know.

What if there were more of them, though? What if, say, *six* Wise Men set out on the adventure, but only three actually made it to the Christ child?

What if two of them had a falling out over something important, like who got to choose where to make camp for the night?

What if one Wise Man insulted another, perhaps inadvertently, and caused the other to throw in the towel?

What if one of them got tired of the trek, missed his family and turned back for home?

What if a couple of them decided they knew a quicker way to reach the star, so they went off on their own and never actually arrived?

What if, because of their inability to deal with each other, some of the original travel team missed out on seeing the Savior with their very own eyes?

When you look around at your life as it exists today, who are your traveling buddies?

Family?
Friends?
Co-workers?
People you worship with?
People you study with?

How long have you been traveling with the same companions? Months? Years? Decades? Longer than you can remember?

There are people we can spend a lifetime with, and there are others who travel with us only for a season. The older I get, the more I recognize the need for both.

Traveling with those who know you well often makes the journey much more enjoyable.

They know what you like, they know how fast you are able to go, and they pretty much know what to expect from you, day in and day out.

Traveling with the familiar is safe. Comfortable.

And it doesn't feel like work.

Traveling with those who are new to you often makes the journey more exciting.

They discover what you like by spending time with you. They figure out how fast you can go by trial and error. They probably have no idea what to expect from you at first, so they pay attention.

Traveling with the yet-to-be-discovered is messy. Enlightening. And it keeps you on your toes.

Sometimes our journey requires more of the familiar. In uncertain situations and difficult times, we need the protection of those who know us well. Sometimes our journey screams for something new, and a jolt to our dead battery can get us rolling down the path with a new perspective, a fresh outlook, and energy to spare.

Star Sighting

I wonder where the Light of Christ is shining over the landscape of your journey today. Is it hovering over the place where you are, or is it twinkling over the mountain and through the woods, beyond the reach of the familiar?

Think about your traveling buddies today…

Does what they bring to the journey fit with what you need along the way?

Do they slow you down or put bounce in your step?

Are they argumentative and bossy, or do they listen when you speak and take great care with your words?

Do they compete with what is important to you, or do they complete that which is important to you?

God often shines His light through those beside us on the trail. If this is where you are today, take time to thank your Father!

But our traveling buddies can also lead us astray. We can get caught up in their bickering, distracted by their issues, annoyed with their bad habits, and frustrated by their need to always be *in charge*, always be *in the lead*, and always be *right*.

If this is where you are today, it's time to look around. It's time to look for those who, like you, are busy looking *up*. When you find them, spend quality time with them. Figure them out by trial and error. Pay attention *to* them and *with* them.

And then, by all means, *move on*.

Daily Giveaway
The dawning of Advent ushers in Christmas card season. We make a list and we check it twice, to be sure we don't leave anyone out.

I believe there is someone you know – a traveling buddy from yesterday or today – whose life would be brighter if you would take the time to send him or her a personal note. Maybe even a Christmas card.

It'll only take a few minutes, but your thoughtfulness and well-chosen words will bring joy to this person who has traveled well with you.

Go ahead. Give some of your love away.

6 *PASSPORT, PLEASE*

Living in southern Arizona provides many opportunities to pass through U.S. Border Patrol and Customs checkpoints. Sometimes the officers just wave me through, but other times I'm obligated to stop as I'm asked the standard questions:

Citizenship?
What is the nature of your business here?
Passport, please.

In other words:

Who are you?
What are you doing here?
Now, prove it.

I've got to giggle when I think about the Wise Men on their journey, passing through countries and over borders for what appears to have been months, if not years, of travel.

What do you suppose their conversations with Border Patrol officials would have sounded like? *Citizenship?* Eastern. Orient. Descendants of the Medes.

What is the nature of your business here? That's a little bit complicated... You see, we're astronomers. We're actually following that star – yes, *that* one. The bright one.

Why? That's a little bit complicated... You see, we think that star is marking the location of a King. We want to find that King and give Him some gifts we've brought along.

What kind of gifts? (You get the idea.)

Passport, please.

Imagine answering those same questions on a similar trek today. Border Patrol would either dismiss us with a roll of the eyes or arrest us, not buying our far-out star story.

Star Sighting
If you think about it, our answer to those same questions *does* sound pretty crazy to those whose feet are anchored in a material world:

Citizenship? Kingdom of God. Heaven.

What is the nature of your business here? That's a little bit complicated... You see, we're actually the hands and feet of Jesus on this earth. Yes, *that* Jesus. Yes, I realize He died a long time ago. But do you realize that He isn't dead? Yes, I realize that no one can see Him. But that's what our work here is all about. Through us, you *can* see Him! No, I'm not saying that I am God. No, I'm not challenging your authority, Sir. (You get the idea.)

Passport, please.

I wonder how *you* would answer these standard questions, in light of your spiritual citizenship?

I propose that the answer you give, and the frequency with which you give it, has the potential to be limitless light in a world filled with lines and boundaries and borders.

The degree to which you are open to letting the Light of God shine through you is the degree to which your life can be a beacon of hope in a desperately hopeless world.

Kind of like the star those adventurous Wise Men were following. The star itself wasn't the thing, but it did serve to capture their attention and draw them *to* the thing itself – to the location of the Savior of the world.

I don't know about you, but I want to *be* that star; capturing the attention of others and drawing them to the Savior Himself!

After all, there was no talk of the star after the Wise Men reached the Christ child.

May there be no talk of me, either, once the true source of the Light has been found.

Daily Giveaway
Our human nature craves attention, doesn't it? It seems our natural *default setting* is to do and say things that put the focus on ourselves.

Today, consider what it would look like to give away the attention we normally like to receive. What would it take for you to shift the focus from *you* onto *God*?

Today, choose *one thing* to do differently and, by making this change, watch how God's love shines through and makes you disappear.

Journal the Journey
Why not share your response to today's Daily Giveaway, and to the Trek so far? Your comments will make our shared experience even richer.

Post a comment at the Pink Shoes Ministries' blog: <u>pinkshoesministries.me</u>

Click on *Trek to the Manger* to share your thoughts!

7 THEY SAY IT'S YOUR BIRTHDAY

Each year as I grow older, more light appears on my cake in the form of an additional candle. I suppose at some point our children decide to forego the fire hazard; maybe because counting the growing number of candles becomes tedious, or maybe because they reach the bittersweet realization that as our years in this world *increase*, the number of birthdays we've yet to celebrate *decrease*.

Either way, when a full-candle salute is given in celebration of a birthday, *light shines*.

This Trek we're on – this Trek to the Manger – is a journey to meet our Savior for the distinct purpose of celebrating *His* birth. Do you remember how much you loved going to a birthday party as a child? Always cake, always ice cream, always party games (and in Arizona, always a piñata). Always so much fun!

Although our celebration rituals change as we grow, most of us still love a good party - especially a birthday party for someone whose life has made our own years more full, more rich, and more blessed.

I believe the reason we love birthdays so much, and the reason we love Christmas so much, is that we are hard-wired to party!

2 Corinthians 5:5-6 tells us:

"We've been given a glimpse of the real thing, our true home, our resurrection bodies! The Spirit of God whets our appetite by giving us a taste of what's ahead. He puts a little of heaven in our hearts so that we'll never settle for less. That's why we live with such good cheer."
(the Message)

Woven into our spiritual DNA is the anticipation of the *ultimate* party – the wedding feast of the Lamb. When that party begins, we will sit at the table with Christ and celebrate new-life-realized in such a way that can only be *glimpsed* in the material reality of here and now.

When we celebrate a birthday, and as we head into celebrations of Christ's human birth, God gives us a taste of what's in store for those who long for Him; those who are seeking Him; those who are willing to stay the course of the journey, no matter how tedious, dusty, and draining the Trek may be.

Star Sighting
What *about* those birthday candles?

I have a dear friend who celebrated more than 80 years of life before her earthly trek ended. Her life was truly a *light* to me, illuminating God's words and ways as together we attempted to stay the course.

My friend Clareen would absolutely *shine* the true Light of the world by allowing Him to create new life inside of her, right up to her home-going day. That God-given life prompted her to create breathtaking art and poetry, which served to capture the attention of people and draw them closer to our creative God.

Her humility and dignity as a daughter of the King were a beautiful illustration of Kingdom life on this earth. Each year she lived allowed God to shine that much more light into the world around her.

Like Clareen, I want my life to burn more brightly with each passing year. Candles on the cake notwithstanding, I want people to see God-breathed Spirit-fire in my words and actions, in greater measure, each year He gives me to live.

Today, may you choose to live in the light of the power of God, who placed His star in the sky so the Wise Men could find their way to Him. May you choose to trust that the God who formed you has plans for you, both in this life *and* the new life that comes with increasing speed as we celebrate each birthday.

Daily Giveaway

Remember when you celebrated your birthday as a child? When my children were growing up, their teachers invited them to bring cupcakes to school on their birthdays - to share with their classmates.

This week, in celebration of our shared spiritual birthday and in anticipation of the birth of Christ, why not make or buy a batch of cupcakes to give away?

Be sure to put a candle in each cupcake – a sign of the Light you have seen and long to share with those you love.

8 SPIRITUAL SELF DEFENSE

Several years ago I took a self defense class with women from my church. What we learned prepared us to defend ourselves from an attack by an enemy. Sometimes these enemies are burglars and thieves, seeking to take something that belongs to us. Sometimes these enemies are predators who care nothing about their victims; they only seek to use their perceived power to get what they want. Sometimes our enemies are people who are desperate for something and are willing to do just about anything to get it.

The Scriptures are quick to remind us that God has an enemy, too. Sometimes God's enemy is a burglar or a thief, seeking to take something that rightfully belongs to Him. Sometimes God's enemy throws his perceived power around, violating God's people and caring nothing about those he chooses to victimize. Sometimes God's enemy is desperate for something that is not his – maybe our *worship*, maybe our *attention*, maybe our *value and importance* in the Kingdom of God - and in his state of desperation, God's enemy is willing to do just about anything to get it.

It's no secret that attacks from God's enemy tend to increase during Advent. With this season comes ample opportunity to attack by way of *strategic distractions* which are, for many of us, out of control from Thanksgiving through New Year's Day. This clever enemy knows that our schedules will be insanely busy, our finances limited and stretched, and our thoughts muddied by stress, worry and loneliness – all of which tend toward a season of darkness rather than a season of *light*.

Star Sighting

Romans 13:12 provides food for thought as this season of Advent begins:

"The night is almost over, and the day is near. So we should get rid of the things that belong to the dark and take up the weapons that belong to the light."
(GW)

Before facing any kind of attack, some instruction on the front end is a good idea (especially where weapons are concerned). In physical self defense, the first lesson we learn is to *be alert*.

It may sound like a no-brainer, but your first line of defense is to *be aware* of your surroundings. Keep your head up and eyes open, watching for warning signs around you. Being present in the moment (rather than lost in the thoughts inside your head) will help you spot hazardous situations before they involve you. Knowing what to look for - a person standing in the dark, around a corner or beside a bush, or a car parked right next to yours when you leave the store at night - can go a long way toward preventing situations from happening at all.

Being prepared and knowing what to look for is a really big deal in physical self defense. There are so many things you can do to keep from becoming a victim! Things like:

Parking under or near lights in the parking lot.

Looking at people who are standing or walking nearby, so they know you have seen them and may be able to identify them if they were to attack.

Walking purposefully, like you're on your way to meet someone, even when you've lost your car in the parking lot.

Spiritually as well as physically, we have to be aware of our surroundings and *be present* to what is happening now.

Being prepared and knowing what to look for is a really big deal in spiritual self defense, too. There are so many things you can do in order to keep from becoming a victim! Things like:

Avoiding empty materialism by planning ahead for meaningful gift-giving with family and friends.

Setting a reasonable gifting budget.

Putting boundaries around your use of time that allow you to be selective about holiday events and gatherings, choosing those which are life giving rather than energy draining.

Surrounding yourself with reminders of the real focus of the Advent season - that God became human and chose to join us here.

The more purposeful you are about moving through Advent toward the manger, the less likely you'll be sidetracked along the way.

Daily Giveaway

Like the sound of the Salvation Army bells that began ringing this week – or like the unsettling buzz of your alarm clock in the morning - let this introductory lesson in self defense wake you up today!

Tune out the lullabies of the enemy!
Stop hitting the snooze button!
Walk toward the light of the Lord!

His armor is within reach, and it has been custom-made to fit and protect you. Where there is no threat, there is no need for armor. The fact that God offers weapons at all is a pretty good sign we'll be needing them. The instruction Book for that armor is also within your reach (probably on your bookshelf at home), and it is filled with insight and truth to help you navigate this Trek to the Manger.

There is a victim mentality at work in this world that doesn't serve us (or God) very well.

Today, let's give away the behaviors that make us easy targets for our physical *and* spiritual enemies.

Yes, there is darkness.
Yes, there is danger.
But thanks be to God – there is also a Savior!

May His rescue reach you today.

9 *(ALMOST) DERAILED*

I was sitting in my car at school, waiting for my son to be dismissed. I had parked in a fairly tight spot, but then *every* spot in the school parking lot is tight at 2:45pm on a Thursday afternoon.

A family walked over to the large truck parked beside me and opened the doors to climb in. I could see how close the truck's rear passenger door was to my shiny new car and I clenched my teeth a bit, waiting for the passengers to load up. After a minute or so, I saw the rear door begin to close and I exhaled with a relieved sigh.

Too soon, apparently, as a book fell out of the vehicle and a passenger swung the door open hard to jump out and retrieve it. *Whack!* My little Cube shook.

Now, you know that I'm on this Advent journey *with* you, right? I have been fixing my eyes on the Light, just like you. I have been looking for ways to bring joy to those around me, just like you. But as I sat in my car as it received its first sizeable door ding, I was almost derailed. I looked back through the rearview mirror first, without turning around in my seat. The adults in the truck noticed that I had noticed, but no one said "I'm sorry." No one got out to look at how much damage had been done.

A passenger picked up the fallen book, shut the door, and they hurriedly drove away. As much as I wanted to survey the damage, I waited until they were several cars past me before I got out to take a look. Paint flaked off the dented spot when I touched it. I was not a happy camper. I shook my head, hands on my hips (attitude stance) as the truck pulled out of the parking lot. My good cheer and tidings of great joy were instantly dashed. I climbed back into the car, almost derailed.

Almost, but not quite.

What happened next can hardly be described. It was almost as if I was an observer while something inside of me worked *against* myself to defuse the emotional reaction brewing inside. Each point of frustration about what had just happened was somehow countered with a voice of peace and understanding.

By the time the school bell rang five minutes later, I stepped out of my car and realized that it was already over inside of me – this potentially ugly derailment.

I had already moved on.

Star Sighting

At this point in the story, it's important for you to know this is *not* normal for me! I can easily remember times when similar situations lit a fire in my head that burned for days.

No, something very different has happened here, and I suspect it's part of the journey. You see, part of me really wanted to jump angrily out of my car and react (badly) to what had taken place, in spite of knowing God would have a better way for me to respond. It's the age-old war between my sinful nature and the counter-cultural ways of God.

Listen to the Apostle Paul as he tries to put this very thing into words:

"Anyone, of course, who has not welcomed this invisible but clearly present God, the Spirit of Christ, won't know what we're talking about. But for you who welcome him, in whom he dwells – even though you still experience all the limitations of sin – you yourself experience life on God's terms... The best thing to do is give [this old life] a decent burial and get on with your new life. God's Spirit beckons. There are things to do and places to go!"
Romans 8: 13-14 *(The Message)*

When life threatens to derail your Trek to the Manger, breathe *in* the Spirit of God and breathe *out* all the rest.

When situations threaten to bring out the worst in you, trust the living Spirit of Christ in you and embrace what He does instead.

Maybe you'll realize in one glorious, illuminating moment that His life has taken root and His Spirit beckons! We have places to go! Things to do! It's time to move on.

Daily Giveaway

With its heightened stress and busyness, this season we're in opens doors to all sorts of potential derailment for those of us who are following God's Light.

It may sound bizarre to you, but I propose that our Daily Giveaway for today be a funeral. A decent burial for that old life and its attention-diverting ways.

Take a few minutes today to jot down the dead things you need to bury.

Take your list and bury it (in the trash can, in the fireplace, or in the shredder). Use Paul's well-spoken words from Romans 8 as a eulogy, and then *walk away*.

10 *WINDOW WASHING*

The window over my kitchen sink *really* needs to be washed. Water splashes onto it while I'm doing the dishes and leaves spots everywhere. Fingerprints and nose prints from the outside, looking in, have smudged the view of my backyard. It's something that needs desperately to be done, but I keep putting it off.

"Your eyes are windows into your body. If you open your eyes wide in wonder and belief, your body fills up with light. If you live squinty-eyed in greed and distrust, your body is a dank cellar. If you pull the blinds on your windows, what a dark life you will have!"
Matthew 6:22-23 *(The Message)*

Star Sighting
Keeping our windows clean takes work. Keeping our windows clean takes time. But having clean windows greatly improves the clarity and enjoyment of the view, doesn't it?

Jesus is reminding us the same is true of the windows through which we view the world: our *eyes*. If the Wise Men had lived greedy, squinty-eyed lives, there is no way they would have given up months – maybe years – of their livelihood to make the Trek to the Manger. They wouldn't have seen the significance of the star. They wouldn't have trusted their God-given instinct or taken one step down the path of uncertainty. They would have stayed home.

Some of us have eyes in need of a good saline flush. Some of us have eyes that are bloodshot red and travel-weary. Some of us have eyes that itch and water and annoy us so much that we tend to look *at* them more than we look *through* them.

Some of us need desperately to follow in the footsteps of the Wise Men, who chose to live with eyes wide open in wonder and belief as they put one foot in front of the other, day in and day out.

The problem is that for some of us, when we open our eyes wide, we just don't like what we see. It's easier sometimes to squeeze our eyes shut tight than to look in the face of brokenness, tragedy, disappointment, and trials.

Who really *wants* to see this world clearly? One look at the newspaper is all it takes some days to convince me to stay home and curl up on the couch with a benign fiction book. Yet Jesus says that when we open our eyes wide, what will fill us up is *light*, not the darkness of the world around us.

Does this even make *sense*? Doesn't Jesus know how much pain we see when we look around? Doesn't He see the messes we make and fail to clean up?

Doesn't He know how inconvenient it is to climb up over the kitchen sink and wipe those windows clean?

Daily Giveaway
For many of us, having a pile of presents under the tree is *tradition*. As Christian parents who are trying to keep the focus on Christ during the holidays, we feel a tug to minimize the gift-giving, don't we? To make less of the *stuff* and more of the *Savior* – which, of course, makes perfect sense. But...

Presents speak a language all their own to our sense of wide-eyed wonder!

Wonder itself is stimulated by a beautifully wrapped gift that remains a mystery until the paper is peeled away on Christmas morning! Maybe the struggle we face isn't the *idea* of gifting, but the *content* of the packages we wrap.

Gifts encourage childlike wonder!
So do surprises.
So do things that are big and awesome,

mysterious and unexplainable.

Maybe we need to become more like our children this Advent season, in order to experience the wonder Jesus is talking about.

For your Giveaway today, there are two suggestions I'd like to make:

Wrap your gifts in amazing ways this season!
Even the gifts for the adults on your list! I know, gift bags are so much easier, but where's the fun in opening *that*? Consider buying a roll of butcher paper or an end roll of newsprint from your local newspaper. Roll it out on the driveway and let your kids or grandkids *paint* and *color* and *decorate* it! Use it to wrap all of your packages for Christmas, adding bows, ribbons, color, sparkle, and *shine*! Increase the wonder-factor for your family this year, if only in this simple way.

Follow a child around for a day!
You can borrow one for a couple of hours if you don't have a small one of your own! Pay attention to how they *see* things. What captures their imagination? What makes them giggle? What makes them say "Wow"?

Determine to adopt some child-like perspective for the rest of this Advent season!

Relish simple pleasures, like cookie baking and decorating. Take a nap! Sit beside the fireplace and roast marshmallows for S'mores. Play outside (in the snow, if you have some).

Hey – whatever washes your windows!

Whatever keeps you wide-eyed and believing in a God whose Kingdom is for those who have become like children – *again*.

11 SPACE CADETS

When I was growing up, it wasn't really a compliment to tell someone they were acting like a *Space Cadet*. It meant *you're kind of dizzy. Out there. Spacey.* You might say it with a joking tone to someone you actually liked, but you probably meant it just the same.

In a spirit of fun, I used to buy Air Head candy by the case when I worked at the YMCA. I kept them in my desk until a staff member did something deserving of the famed *Air Head Award*, at which time I would present the candy to the Space Cadet who had earned it. All in good fun, mind you, but also in earnest. After all, until we face our mistakes and limitations head on, we won't be moving forward anytime soon.

These days I'm revisiting the definition of *Space Cadet*. God's Word has captured my attention on the topic with this passage from 2 Corinthians 6:11-13:

"...I can't tell you how much I long for you to enter this wide-open, spacious life. We didn't fence you in. The smallness you feel comes from within you. Your lives aren't small, but you're living them in a small

way. I'm speaking as plainly as I can and with great affection. Open up your lives. Live openly and expansively!"
(The Message)

Star Sighting
As the Wise Men traveled the road to the Christ child, there must have been moments in the wide, open countryside when they thought...
We are so very small.

You can relate, can't you? Remember the last time you sat outside on a starry night and took stock of how immense the sky is, and how small you are in comparison?

What if God sent the Wise Men on this lengthy trek not *only* to introduce them to His Son? What if He had something else in mind for these scholar-astronomers? I wonder if God was calling the Wise Men to be the first *Space Cadets* in the Kingdom of God?

Space Cadets in the sense that their purpose, goals, and priorities probably looked pretty dizzy to others along the way.

Space Cadets in the sense that God used His own creation – a star set in space – to get their attention and create momentum in their lives along the path of His choosing.

Space Cadets in the sense that, by following His star, these Wise Men joined God in His work of creating space in their lives for the Holy to live, move, and breathe.

Think about your own life. How much space exists in your day, and in your head, for the God of the universe to dwell? Is there ample room for Him to live, move and breathe, or have you so successfully filled your calendar with your *own* purposes, goals, and priorities that there is precious little space in which to entertain the Spirit of God?

The Star Sighting in our lives today is an *actual* star in the sky. One small, insignificant star, made significant by the vastness of the blanket of space in which it resides. When we choose to empty ourselves of worldly concerns, we create space for Christ to move into the neighborhood. When He arrives, we find our painfully small existence exposed to the wide-open, spacious life God has crafted. The life we've already been given through the work of our Messiah on the cross.

In this context, the best we can be this Advent season is a regiment of Space Cadets! People who are so anxious for what God has in store that we willingly create space (in our heads, in our hearts, and in our lives) for God to come alive.

Daily Giveaway

Being a Space Cadet for the Kingdom isn't an easy assignment. Most of us are quite skilled at filling our time with activities and busyness. Most of us can easily get caught up in our *own* issues, memories, and worries about the future, leaving little inhabitable space for the Spirit of God to fill. For some of us, today's Giveaway is going to be the greatest challenge we face on our Trek to the Manger.

Because some of us don't know how to say *no*.

We have said *yes* to many things, but what happens when God's *best* arrives on the scene and we can't squeeze it in because we're already too busy with the *good*?

Take stock of your schedule today. Open up your calendar and read through your commitments. Allow the weight of each one to fall on you afresh.

What feels heavy? What do you dread?
If it feels like a burden, can it be done by someone else?
What do you never seem to tire of doing?
What seems to have a life and energy all its own?

Are you Space Cadet enough to trim away the *good* in order to create space for God's *best*?

12 *SPRINKLES*

Hear these words from Paul today as our Trek to the Manger continues:

"I do want to point out, friends, that time is of the essence. There is no time to waste, so don't complicate your lives unnecessarily. Keep it simple – in marriage, grief, joy, whatever. Even in ordinary things – your daily routines of shopping, and so on. Deal as sparingly as possible with the things the world thrusts on you. This world as you see it is on its way out. I want you to live as free of complications as possible."
1 Corinthians 7:29-32 *(The Message)*

"As free of complications as possible."
Is that even possible?

Perhaps our inability to grasp what Paul is saying is our fondness for what my friend, Nancy Whitney, calls *sprinkles*. In her book, *Now is the Time to Do What You Love*, Nancy explains the benefits of downsizing:

"...most of us are surrounded by 'sprinkles'. Using the analogy of a cake: the cake itself has flavor and so does the frosting. But what do the sprinkles really add? Empty calories. Take a good look around you.

Chances are, you're surrounded by things that you no longer use and likely never will." [1]

Go ahead – do it. Take a good look around the room you're sitting in right now. Think about the space you live in – your shelves, cupboards, and closets.

Can you identify your flavor of *sprinkles*? What are the things that make your proverbial cupcakes look colorful and cute, but fail to add anything of substance to your life? What constitutes empty calories – things you consume that fail to nourish your soul?

Star Sighting

I seriously doubt the Wise Men traveled with sprinkles. I suspect they limited their luggage to the items that provided forms of nourishment, sustenance, and protection for the journey. They had to be footloose enough to keep up with the star!

Personally, I fail the sprinkles test every time I pack for a trip. *I might need this. I could want that. If it's cold... If it rains...* Be honest! You've been there, too. I can't even stomach the thought of going camping because the what-ifs require such an intimidating packing list. Either the stuff goes or the kids go. Both won't fit in the car!

It takes discipline to pack a week's worth of

personal items into a carry-on, and it takes discipline to simplify a life that has been complicated by the stuff of this world. Even as willing recipients of our sprinkles, Nancy Whitney reminds us that *"you expend energy on your possessions. Simplifying your possessions allows you to redirect that energy."*

I don't know about you, but I sure could use some energy to redirect during this Advent season! I could channel it toward the process of becoming a *Space Cadet* – freeing up space in my head and schedule for the Spirit of God to move in and move me. Or maybe my *Traveling Buddies* need some attention, but I haven't been able to carve out the time.

Sprinkle maintenance requires time, energy, and attention that Paul tells us is better spent on the things that matter to God. In fact, Paul says:

"All I want is for you to be able to develop a way of life in which you can spend plenty of time together with the Master without a lot of distractions."
1 Corinthians 7:35 *(The Message)*

Daily Giveaway
I have a dear friend who moved from an enormous house (with loads of sprinkles) into a much smaller home. She was forced to downsize her estate within a very short time frame, creating stress and using up precious energy that

would have been better spent on walking her family through a season of emotional and financial crisis.

I can't help but wonder what might happen if we would choose to *live* as the Wise Men *traveled*, limiting our possessions to those that provide nourishment, sustenance, and protection for the life-journey we are on.

Wouldn't it be a great relief if we could keep life simple and be footloose enough to travel as the Spirit leads?

Today, take stock of your sprinkles.

Pay close attention to those possessions that drain your resources – time, energy, and money. Consider asking God to help you give away these empty calories (or maybe even sell them on Craigslist), not so you can turn around and sprinkle a new variety of colors on your cake, but so you can direct much needed energy toward spending time with the One who gave up *everything* for you.

13 A NEW GENERATION OF TREKKIES

Amazing things happen on the road!

You might disagree, and I wouldn't fault you. Most of us are keener on arriving at our destination than buckling ourselves (and our kids and our dogs) into the car for a road trip. We'd just as soon click our ruby red heels together three times and find ourselves sitting at Grandma's dinner table than facing scary holiday traffic, potential weather complications, and lines of bitter complaining at TSA checkpoints.

In a culture that demands instant gratification, journeys rarely bring joy.

Star Sighting
Much of what we read in Scripture happened on the road. Conversations, miracles, and teaching quite often took place while people were moving from one location to the next. Three stories stand out to me as Star Sightings today – examples of the amazing work God can do on the journey.

On the road to Damascus, an angry church bully

set out to silence the followers of a Jewish rabbi, whose community of faith was called *The Way*. Never mind that these followers claimed their rabbi had returned from the dead. Never mind that they believed He was actually God. Never mind that they claimed He had returned bodily to Heaven by way of the sky above a Bethany hillside. Saul was bound and determined to do some damage to *The Way* by rounding up the most outspoken groupies and throwing them in jail.

In his mind, Saul's destination was crystal clear, until the Light showed up and blinded him. On the road to Damascus, this man who breathed hate and destruction caught a lethal dose of the Light of Heaven, and from that point in his journey, everything changed. His heart. His name. His destination. Everything changed because Jesus showed up on the road.

On the road to Emmaus, two grief-stricken followers of the crucified Jesus were traveling away from Jerusalem. Their Lord's body had disappeared from the tomb, and while some of the women in their group claimed He was alive, no one could say for sure. These two travelers were joined on the road by a man who knew much about the prophesied Messiah. He walked with them and talked with them. He taught and encouraged them. And when He sat down to share a meal with them, the Light from Heaven opened their eyes and the Jesus followers recognized their companion as the risen Christ! They said to each other:

"It felt like a fire burning in us when Jesus talked to us on the road and explained the Scriptures to us." Luke 24:32 *(NCV)*

On the road to Gaza, a privileged official of the Ethiopian queen was traveling by chariot. He had gone to Jerusalem to worship and was reading the Scriptures as he traveled home. A follower of Jesus, a man named Philip, was traveling the same road. Prompted by God's Spirit, Philip began a conversation with the eunuch, and one man's journey was drastically altered when he was baptized in a roadside pond. Acts 8:39 tells us that, although Philip disappeared suddenly after the baptism, *"the officer continued on his way home, full of joy."*

Full of joy? *While on the road? While driving home for Christmas? While being full-body-scanned? While sitting in a coffee shop, waiting for the plows to clear the road?*

Full of joy? *While missing loved ones who won't be here this year? While wondering whether you'll have enough money to pay next month's rent? While driving to the clinic for chemo?*

Full of joy? *While feeling so very lonely, so very*

weak, and so very, very tired?

Daily Giveaway
It's easy to be full of joy once we've reached our destination. It's quite another thing to be joyful on the journey, no matter what may happen. No matter what obstacles may come. No matter the potential hazards and risks.

Our ability to experience joy on the road to Heaven is what separates the spiritual girls from the women. It's what sets us apart from a world obsessed with *arriving*. It's what shines the Light of Christ into a watching world. And it calls for a paradigm shift among believers! Our Heavenly destination isn't a distant eternity, but a citizenship that has already begun. A citizenship that began on the road.

A new generation of followers of Christ is being raised up on the highways and byways of this world. Not unlike *The Way*, these believers are ready to leverage their complicated earthly citizenship for the simplicity of following Jesus on the road of *His* choosing. Not blindly following, mind you – even Saul-turned-Paul was given back his sight – but with vision illuminated by the Light of the world.

A new generation of *Trekkies*.

On a Trek to the Manger... and beyond.

14 *HOLY GPS!*

Years ago, my family took a road trip. Traveling through my husband's old stomping grounds in New Mexico, we decided to take the back way into his home town. We had a shiny new, all-wheel drive Subaru and thought this would be a great way to test it out – on a rugged, off-road adventure.

Let's just say that the way was not marked, the road was clearly no longer there, and our rugged off-road adventure left a dent in the side of the Subaru where a stubborn boulder got the better of us.

Did we ask for directions? *No.*
Were there signs of other travelers on the route we chose? *No.*
Would it have been wise to follow the road that was marked, paved, and tried-and-true? *You betcha.*

This is what the Lord says:

"Stand at the crossroads and look; ask for the ancient paths, ask where the good way is, and walk in it, and

you will find rest for your souls."
Jeremiah 6:16 *(NIV)*

The Message says it this way:

"Ask for directions to the old road."

Great advice. Wish we had thought of that.

Star Sighting
God's Word on this matter is pretty clear. Asking for directions on our spiritual Trek is not only a good idea, it's a *must*. Not only that, but when we choose to ignore God's tried-and-true, mapping out our own route instead, disaster and dented fenders are in store.

"I even appointed watchmen over you and said, 'Listen to the sound of the trumpet!' But you said, 'We will not listen.'"
Jeremiah 6:17 *(NIV)*

God goes to great lengths to keep us on the narrow road! His alarms are sounding when we stray, alerting us to His presence and directing us back to the ancient path of faith. Spiritual rumble strips, you might say. Yet none of these do any good if we choose to ignore the signs.

Even the star in the sky would have failed to deliver the Wise Men to their destination if they had chosen to ignore it.

God's Word tells us that *if* we pay attention and keep our eyes on the road, and *if* we ask for directions when we find we've lost our way, and *if* we choose to follow His directions when He provides them, *then* we will find rest for our souls.

The problem is, I don't always pay attention.

Sometimes I miss my turn for all the distractions in my life. Sometimes I fail to ask God for directions and instead blaze my own poorly planned trail over hazardous terrain (with fierce boulders that spring up out of nowhere). There are times when I *do* ask for directions, but instead of asking God, I ask the guy at the gas station or a friend from church - taking greater stock in the words and suggestions of people than I do in the Word of God Himself.

Daily Giveaway

God, in His great love for us, has given us a holy GPS – a spiritual positioning system of sorts – in the pages of His Word. It's not so much a road map as it is a way of finding ourselves in relationship to Him.

GPS uses longitude and latitude to place us in our current location on the globe. God's Word uses His unchanging truth and our unfolding response to place us in our current location on a spiritual grid. No matter where you are. Even when you have no idea where you are, God's Word can show you.

Then you can rest.

And for some of us, rest would be a welcome destination to reach.

As we decisively choose to give away our efforts at self-guidance and self-help, consider carefully the other voices we listen to.

Ask God to help you identify any source of information that is inconsistent with His holy GPS.

Any voice that seeks to direct your thoughts and actions in a way that fails to recognize the authority of God is in conflict with His Word and may very well mislead you. That voice may even be your own.

Conserve your energy, my friend. You're going to need it.

This Trek isn't over yet.

15 *(SPIRITUALLY) HOMELESS*

Homelessness in America is undoubtedly a growing concern for many of us on this Trek to the Manger. While most of us are not personally affected by the statistics, we probably know people for whom the following numbers represent more than an issue, but their own harsh reality:

15 percent of Americans live in poverty, including one in five children, the highest rate in the industrialized world.

42 percent of homeless children are under the age of 6.

Almost 60 percent of Americans will spend at least one year below the poverty line at some point between ages 25 and 75.

There is no city or county anywhere in the United States where a worker making the minimum wage can afford a fair market rate one-bedroom apartment.[2]

According to the US Department of Housing and Urban Development, there were 633,782 sheltered and unsheltered homeless persons nationwide on a single night in January 2012.[3]

The numbers are heartrending and growing. More and more people in the land of the free are moving back in with Mom and Dad (if Mom and Dad still have a home) or onto the streets, where they may be homeless but are definitely *not* alone.

When we look around our communities, we find pockets of people who are reaching out to the homeless. There are organizations providing shelter, counseling, and job skills training. There are soup kitchens and clothing projects designed to meet the most basic of human needs. There are those who are getting their hands dirty by building low-income housing for families in desperate need of a safe, warm place. With all of the activity going on in these areas, it's pretty easy to dismiss the problem (it isn't *my* problem, after all) and walk on by.

Not unlike what we do every day with the *spiritually* homeless.

Who are the spiritually homeless, you ask? The American Religious Identification Survey (ARIS), released in March 2008, found a significant decline in religion and a rise in secularism that set news outlets buzzing.

"More than ever before, people are just making up their own stories of who they are. They say, 'I'm everything. I'm nothing. I believe in myself,' says Barry Kosmin, survey co-author."

According to the ARIS, 15 percent of Americans claim to subscribe to no religion at all. In spite of the addition of 50 million adults to the U.S. population since 1990, nearly every religious denomination in our country is losing ground.[4]

Star Sighting

You may be thinking this is *not* where you wanted to go on our Trek today. Well, me neither. In fact, I've struggled with every word written this morning because this topic isn't *light*.

I really would prefer to let someone else deal with it so I can get on with my to-do list for today. I've got places to go and people to see, just like you.

God stops me in my self-righteous tracks, however, with these words from James 5:19-20:

"My dear friends, if you know people who have wandered off from God's truth, don't write them off. Go after them. Get them back and you will have rescued precious lives from destruction and prevented an epidemic of wandering away from God."
(The Message)

God is giving you and me, His *Trekkies*, an opportunity to join in His redemptive work of rescue! There are precious people who are wandering around, spiritually homeless, in our neighborhoods and communities right now. And while it may seem completely overwhelming and seriously impossible for us to reach *all* of the wandering homeless, you can rest assured that is not what He is asking us to do.

Daily Giveaway

If you give away anything on this Trek to the Manger day, give away *this*: your tendency to walk on by the homeless (spiritually or physically) and do nothing at all. Instead:

When you hit the drive-thru for a burger at lunch, why not buy and give a second one away to someone who could use the nourishment?

Redeem those points on your credit cards for gift cards to local stores where food and clothing can be bought. Give away the gift cards as God gives you opportunity!

Keep a cooler of snacks in your car to share with the sign-carrying, newspaper-selling folks on the side of the road. Plan ahead. Make a difference in a precious life today.

For the spiritually homeless, well, that depends on who you know. Maybe your Giveaway is a card or an email aimed at reconnecting with someone who needs to know they are loved. For those who are close by, perhaps a hug or handshake is in order.

Whatever you do, go after them!

Don't wait for them to come to you.

[2] FAMILY PROMISE: HTTP://WWW.FAMILYPROMISE.ORG/FAST-FACTS

[3] US DEPARTMENT OF HOUSING AND URBAN DEVELOPMENT,

HTTP://PORTAL.HUD.GOV/HUDPORTAL/HUD?SRC=/PRESS/PRESS_RELEASES_

MEDIA_ADVISORIES/2012/HUDNO.12-191

[4] "MOST RELIGIOUS GROUPS IN USA HAVE LOST GROUND, SURVEY FINDS" BY

CATHY LYNN GROSSMAN, USA TODAY

HTTP://USATODAY30.USATODAY.COM/NEWS/RELIGION/2009-03-09-

AMERICAN-RELIGION-ARIS_N.HTM

16 *TEND TO YOUR KNITTING*

We've got our hands full these days, don't we? Looking at our proverbial plates, no one is going hungry here – at least not when it comes to the smorgasbord of *activity*. Family gatherings. Christmas programs and parties. Shopping and cleaning and shuttling the kids around town.

My plate is full – how about yours?

With so much of my own house to keep, I'm stunned every time I see people crossing the line – stepping outside of the work of their own hands to pass judgment or criticize another. I can hardly keep track of my *own* collection of hats, let alone follow others to see how they handle their assortment of roles as parent, friend, caregiver, employee, or co-worker.

Even when I *do* notice the shortcomings of those around me, which is unavoidable at times, I find I'm asking God to shine the Light of His Word as a filter for my thoughts.

A filter for my *tongue*.

Star Sighting

Chapter 14 in the book of Romans is rich with filters for believers on a Trek to the Manger. Words like these provide imperfect *me* with some desperately needed perspective when it comes to my role as co-sojourner on the Path:

"It's God we are answerable to – all the way from life to death and everything in between – not each other. That's why Jesus lived and died and then lived again: so that he could be our Master across the entire range of life and death, and free us from the petty tyrannies of each other... So tend to your knitting. You've got your hands full just taking care of your own life before God."

Romans 14:7-9, 13 *(The Message)*

Some of us need to be freed from the petty tyrannies of each other - even the pettiness of our brothers and sisters in Christ.

And some of us need to free others from the petty tyranny of ourselves. Our judgment. Our careless comments. Our lack of respect and sensitivity.

"Your task is to single-mindedly serve Christ. Do that and you'll kill two birds with one stone: pleasing the God above you and proving your worth to the people around you."

Romans 14:18 *(The Message)*

Apparently it's not our job to comment on how others serve Christ, or point out what we would do differently, or draw attention to their obvious mistakes and poor decisions.

Too often we exercise a critical spirit toward others, casting shadows their way rather than getting out of God's way and allowing His Light to shine.

Too often we fail to tend to our knitting, to the detriment of precious others who need a beacon to move toward, not a black hole to fall into.

Daily Giveaway
For the days that remain on our Trek to the Manger, I invite you to put this mantra before you at every turn:

How can I serve Jesus today?

After all, we move toward what we focus on, and when we focus on Christ we can't help but be drawn into closer relationship with His Spirit. By giving away our need to meddle and make ourselves feel better at the expense of another, we take on a *bearable* yoke – the yoke of a Savior who promised to not weigh us down.

We're already – all of us – carrying a load of worry, disappointment, and questions about our lives in this broken world. It was never God's intent that we would add weight to the load of others. Why would we (why *do* we?) weigh others down when God has clearly called us to ease one another's burdens rather than *become* a burden as we walk through life together?

"So let's agree to use all our energy in getting along with each other. Help others with encouraging words; don't drag them down by finding fault."
Romans 14:19 *(The Message)*

Giving away every focus *but* Christ, we join those who are busily knitting - doing our creative best with the work God has given us to do.

Today, let's choose to pour our energy into restoring and mending, caring and carrying others by the power of the Spirit of the Christ child Himself.

I don't know about you, but *that's* a sweater (or hat or scarf) that goes with everything in my closet!

I can't wait to put it on.

17 PURPOSEFUL ACTS OF KINDNESS

In the film *Evan Almighty*,[5] Morgan Freeman's God character promotes the worthiness of *random acts of kindness*. You've probably heard this phrase before. In certain Christian circles, this mantra has made the rounds many times – it's the idea of surprising people with unexpected expressions of care and concern.

Who doesn't want to be surprised by the generosity and thoughtfulness of others? Kindness is a beautiful thing! The problem is, the word *random* implies *inconsistent. Convenient. Sporadic. Unpredictable.*

I don't think this is exactly what God has in mind for communicating His love in action.

Star Sighting

"Watch what God does, and then you do it, like children who learn proper behavior from their parents. Mostly what God does is love you. Keep company with him and learn a life of love. Observe how Christ loved us. His love was not cautious but extravagant. He didn't love in order to get something

from us but to give everything of himself to us. Love like that."
Ephesians 5:1-2 *(The Message)*

While your *random* kind acts toward others may communicate God's love, what they don't do is reflect a life that is growing every day in relationship with the Author of love itself.

If we were to take to heart these words of Paul to the Ephesians, we would walk away from *random* and embrace a life of *purposeful* acts of generosity and extravagant love.

To love like Christ isn't random or put on display through occasional bursts of good will.

To love like Christ is to give everything of ourselves, expecting nothing in return.

Not only when we *feel* like loving. Not only when our love can be shared in *surprising* ways.

When we learn to love as God loves us, we love: *Consistently. Predictably. Unselfishly. Unconditionally.*

Unlike a strobe light, characterized by darkness between flashes of light, God-taught love shines steady and true. It's always there.

Always on display.

A candle in the window, calling weary travelers, "Come home."

Daily Giveaway

When I was a Girl Scout leader, my troop took great pleasure in spending the proceeds from our annual cookie sales. Often we would go on an outing together – one year we had a tea party at a local restaurant, dressing up in formal gowns with hats, shoes, and handbags. Another time we went to the local beauty college and had up dos before going out to lunch together. Nearly every year, though, we set out to use a chunk of our cookie *dough* on a special project. We became *Secret Angels*.

This was one of our favorite outings! Each girl would select a person or family she knew was in need of something (encouragement, a smile, or help with a financial need). With $10 in each girl's pocket, we explored a local dollar store where each one purchased gifts to give to the recipient(s) they chose. What followed was a gift wrapping party, where beautiful bags and baskets were created. The girls prepared cards to go with their gifts, and each one left with instructions on how to complete their *Secret Angel* assignment.

Each year these gifts were given anonymously. Part of the fun was to quietly place her gift on the doorstep and ring the bell, then run away (giggling, of course) in an attempt to keep her identity a secret.

Today I invite you to slip into a pair of angel wings and reach out quietly to someone in your life who needs a touch from God.

You know someone who is struggling with the season.
You know someone who struggles financially.
You know someone who thinks they've been forgotten.

Being a *Secret Angel* doesn't require an expensive gift or your ability to ring a doorbell and run like the wind. The only needful thing is that you choose, on purpose, to extend the love you're learning to someone else. Today.

And then tomorrow, do it again.

[5] *EVAN ALMIGHTY*, 2007 UNIVERSAL PICTURES

18 9 1/2 MILES PER HOUR

Jesus prayed for His disciples:

"Holy Father, keep them safe by the power of your name, the name you gave me, so that they will be one, just as you and I are one."
John 17:11b *(NCV)*

How hard is it for people to be *one* - completely unified in heart and mind? Is Jesus praying an impossible prayer?

Star Sighting
I took a trip to San Francisco with my family. In the midst of a whirlwind tour of the Bay, among the crowds of tourists and slightly annoyed locals, God gave me a surprising glimpse of this idea of *oneness*... And it starts with a car. You, behind the wheel of a car, which for most of us is a picture of independence, freedom of choice, and control.

Christians tend to live their spiritual lives the way Americans live their daily lives. We jump in the car, go *where* we want and need to go *when* we want and need to go there, and then we go home. All of us moving in different directions, at different times, on different routes, based on what suits us best.

Enter here - the San Francisco Cable Car. Not to be confused with a tram or a trolley (though they may look a lot the same on the outside), a Cable Car is completely unique in the way that it works.

First of all, a Cable Car does not have its own power source. There is no motor inside the vehicle! On its own, it's nothing more than a nifty looking car that isn't going *anywhere* anytime soon.

Secondly, a Cable Car runs on a specific path. This route was pre-determined when the tracks were put in place, and there aren't options like "*hang a left at the next block*" unless the track already goes that way. You might say this track is narrow, and there is no doubt as to where it leads.

Also, a Cable Car has lots of room for different kinds of passengers. You can sit inside if you don't want to be windblown or get wet when it's raining. You can stand in the back and have a great view of what's behind, or sit in front to see what's coming up ahead. People on the sides enjoy the open air and can experience the city as it goes by, and frequent stops allow new people to jump on and others to climb off.

There is a limit to the number of passengers who can ride at one time, though, because the car won't operate correctly with too much weight or too many bodies on board.

What makes a Cable Car move? Where is the power if not in the car itself? This was a Star Sighting for me – walking across the street, over the tracks, and hearing the steady hum of the cable moving underneath. That cable is *always* in motion. When a Cable Car is stopped, it's because the car has become disconnected from the cable, but the cable itself does not stop. When the car is moving, it's because it is connected to the cable.

On the streets of San Francisco, there are multiple Cable Cars in various locations on any given route, but the moment one of those cars connects to the cable, it is going the *same speed* as every other car along the path. This is because the cable itself is always moving at 9 ½ miles per hour. There is no *fast car* or *slow car* on this route – the cable keeps things steady and reliable, and the speed of the cable is always the same.

Cable Cars share the road with other traffic, too. While we were riding, there were cars zipping around all over the streets where the tracks were laid, honking at the Cable Cars while going their own speed, making their own way.

Believe it or not, it was here where a vision of *achievable unity* among Jesus' followers began to develop, like a Polaroid picture exposed to the light.

There are authentic Cable Cars and authentic families of faith. They don't just *look* like the real thing, but they are genuine in both design and function.

An authentic Cable Car, like the authentic Christian church, has no power in itself. Only when connected to the steady cable - to the power of the living God - can there be any movement or progress made.

The Cable Car designer laid the tracks and there is no doubt as to where they lead. You can be sure that "wide is the road that leads to destruction", but if you want to take that route, you're going to need to step off of the Cable Car and climb into your Ford; we who are on board know where this track leads!

There is more than one Cable Car on the tracks (and more than one church on the block), traveling the same route. A variety of people are riding in each car, and sometimes they come, sometimes they go. Sometimes, they switch cars. Yet all are on the same path as long as we get into the car.

There can only be so many bodies on the Cable Car before the car (and the operator) get stressed. There are limits for safety and proper function of the car, and of the church.

If a Cable Car stops its forward progress, it's because the operator and passengers made the decision to stop. The cable keeps going, and so does God.

Every car connected to the cable will go the same speed, full speed ahead, at 9 ½ mph. That's the speed of the cable. No one can boast that their car is faster and covering more ground, or that their car is slower, allowing more passengers to jump on.

God – like the cable – remains the same.

Daily Giveaway
The cost of unity among travelers on this road may very well be *control*. As long as I insist on doing what I want to do, I find myself at odds with others around me who are doing the same.

Cable car or not, even the Wise Men would have suffered the effects had one or more of them acted on their internal control freak rather than sharing the journey with one another.

Today isn't the first on this Trek to the Manger where the Daily Giveaway is *control*. Instead of creating your own energy, try standing still for a moment on the road.

Can you feel the vibration of the movement of the Spirit?

Do you hear the hum of activity in the Kingdom of God?

Will you look up to see the light of the star, beckoning you toward the common destination it illuminates?

There's a Cable Car loading on a busy street near you! It may cost you some independence, but I assure you that with the Spirit of God on board, it'll be one heck of a memorable ride.

19 99 *BOTTLES OF BEER ON THE WALL*

Visions of yellow school buses dance in my head as the words of the classic traveling song come to mind:

99 bottles of beer on the wall
99 bottles of beer
Take one down, pass it around
98 bottles of beer on the wall.

One such trip was with my 5th grade class in Tucson, AZ. A day trip to Colossal Cave. I have a vivid memory of being bounced in my seat as the rolling road through the desert brought us closer and closer to our underground adventure. We were kids. We had no worries! And we sang at the top of our lungs, holding nothing back -
99 bottles of beer on the wall.

Star Sighting
Traveling songs. Songs for the road. Songs to pass the time. Songs to sing just because we can. For me, it was never about the beer (although I suppose that even *saying* the word beer, let alone singing it over and over again, had some appeal to this 5th grader who wouldn't actually taste the stuff until years later).

For me, singing these words was about sharing the journey with my friends. And loving every minute of it.

Ever wonder how the Wise Men passed the time on their Trek to the Manger?

How about Jesus and His followers – they were on the road a lot. Do you suppose *they* sang traveling songs in between Jesus' teachings and miraculous healings? They were human, after all. And I suppose there were moments when, even for *them*, it was all about sharing the journey with friends. And loving every minute of it.

As a grown-up, I tend to be pretty intense (*shocking – I know*). I've attended 5th grade field trips as a mom and, admittedly, I have cringed when the singing of *99 Bottles* begins. In some circles, they've moved from beer to Coke, but the song is still the same – sung with just as much gusto and vigor as I once had, sitting where they now sit. But to be honest, I don't enjoy it as much anymore.

Several years ago I took a personal retreat. I brought a pile of work along with me – preparations for Vacation Bible School, a group prayer experience I was creating, and lots of inner clutter that desperately needed to be sorted out. I was focused intently on retreating, spending every waking moment involved in actively writing, reading, and praying. Every now and then I'd stop to eat a meal bar, never missing a beat as I immediately returned to my work.

Late afternoon on the second day, I took a walk to the back of the retreat property. I found a labyrinth in the desert landscaping, surrounded by benches and mesquite trees. I had never walked a labyrinth, though I had read about them before. Provided were some basic prompts on subtle signs at the entrance to the path, which I read before entering.

Following the suggestions, I set out to walk toward the center as if I were walking through my life from birth to present day. As I walked, I invited reruns of significant life events to play inside my head, pausing every now and then to smile at a memory or to ask for forgiveness as the weight of my mistakes grew heavy.

I finally reached the center of the path. After a few quiet moments, I resolved to complete my walk, listening to God and following His lead as I let go of the past and welcomed whatever my future might hold (*did I mention that I can be fairly intense?*).

What followed was one of the most intimate and beautiful interactions I have ever had with God. At three points on the journey out of the center, I clearly heard His voice speaking into my life and issues in ways I never had before.

As I neared the exit, I noticed that a rabbit had joined me on the outside edge of the labyrinth, bouncing around playfully. He would hop around, then stop and sit, eyeing me expectantly. After a few minutes, he'd take off into the brush, but he always came back. As if he was waiting for me.

It was cute, though a bit unnerving. As I rounded the last curve and moved toward the path's end, God's final words to me appeared like a brilliant star in the light of day:

Hurry up! Come and PLAY! Hurry up and LIVE!

Have you ever laughed and cried at the same time? The bunny stuck around, though he must've thought I was losing it, and God's message hit the nerve it was intended for. It was there, alone and absorbed in God all by myself, that I realized I was missing the point of my own walk in faith.

Thinking isn't living.
Living is living!

The rich faith-life God longs for us to live is all about sharing the journey with friends.

And loving every minute of it.

Daily Giveaway

"Sing, sing your hearts out to God! Let every detail in your lives – words, actions, whatever – be done in the name of the Master, Jesus, thanking God the Father every step of the way."
Colossians 3:16-17 *(The Message)*

I don't think God cares *how* it sounds – He wants us to sing with a thankful heart every step of the way! He wants us to get out of our heads long enough to realize He has been waiting on us to *hurry up! Come and PLAY! Hurry up and LIVE!*

The neighborhood I live in now has a substantial rabbit population, which I'm quite sure is not accidental but by design. Every time I leave my house, as Peter Rabbit darts behind a tree or into the wash, I'm reminded of the life my Father is calling me to live.

A life where every word and action is done in Jesus' name.

A life filled with joyful noise and grateful response to every good gift from above.

Be reminded today that *you* are God's child! Find a way to connect with the days when life was simple and uncomplicated, then choose to give away a taste of the freedom you have found in Christ.

Give those around you permission to enjoy the life you share.

And maybe even sing a pointless traveling song.

Just because you can.

20 *KINGDOM BUSINESS 101*

I sat at my computer tonight for about ten minutes, filling out online surveys from stores and restaurants I've visited over the past week. It seems *everyone* is seeking feedback from customers – and rewarding that feedback with coupons and discounts.

I'm all for saving money, especially where I do business on a regular basis. The establishments I frequent are those where customer service is a big deal. They know what their products and services are, and they know how to pass them along to me with courtesy and quality. These are the places where my time and money are well spent.

There is one local business, however, that frustrates me every time I walk in the doors. This familiar chain store *never* has what I need, no matter what it is. Even if I search long and hard enough for something that would work in place of what I went in to find, by the time I reach the checkout line there is one, lone cashier whose sense of urgency has already clocked out. And there is a line. Every. Single. Time.

Star Sighting

It's a beautiful thing to walk through the doors of a business where you know you will get what you came for.

Like the mom-and-pop sushi place I love to visit, whose caterpillar rolls are to die for. I may wait awhile for my food to be prepared, but I'm confident every time that what I'm waiting for is exactly what I'm paying for. And it's going to taste amazing, just like it did last week, because they know what they're doing with seaweed and fish.

On this Trek to the Manger, I'm learning that my time is valuable. Like the Wise Men, who sold out to the idea of reaching their well-marked destination, I am completely committed to growing in the knowledge and understanding of the Kingdom of God.

The Wise Men were well-traveled. I want to be well-trained in the thoughts and ways of God. So I study the Scriptures and spend time in His presence. I walk the well-worn path of the seekers before me, whose lives bear the scars of the journey in painfully beautiful ways.

Just like the disciples of Christ, our training while Trekking produces some surprising results:

"...you see how every student well-trained in God's kingdom is like the owner of a general store who can put his hands on anything you need, old or new, exactly when you need it."
Matthew 13:52 *(The Message)*

Physically, I appreciate the store whose employees can put what I need into my hands.

Spiritually, I am amazed by the God who is able to meet my every need, using the hands of ordinary believers who are just like me.

I'll go to those believers for help every time. And so will you. Because the light that shines through a life shaped by Christ helps us to find what we need.

Daily Giveaway

Consider what you appreciate about the stores and restaurants you endorse. What keeps you coming back? What sets those establishments apart from the rest? How do you *feel* walking in and walking out of your favorite businesses? How might you communicate your appreciation to those who work hard to retain your business?

Who do you know that fits the description of a well-trained student of the Kingdom?

What sets them apart from the rest?

How do you feel before and after spending time with him or her?

How might you communicate your appreciation to those who share their Kingdom-wisdom with you?

Today, let's give away some appreciation for the diligent, hard workers in the Kingdom (and the world) around us.

Jesus is teaching Kingdom Business 101, and you've got a full-ride scholarship! Jesus knows exactly what you need, exactly when you need it, and He can put His hands on it at exactly the right time.

And He wants to teach us to do the same.

21 *GIFT SELECTION DAY*

Today was the day. Gift Selection Day.

Working rather loosely with a handwritten list and armed with a stack of coupons, I hit the stores in a last-ditch attempt to find the perfect gift for everyone on my list. It took four hours in half a dozen stores before I was able to place a checkmark beside almost every name. It took four trips from the car to the living room to transfer all of my finds to the to-be-wrapped pile beside the tree. And it will likely take four days to actually *wrap* every one of these carefully chosen treasures!

This is how I get it done, on Gift Selection Day.

Star Sighting
Some of us have taken a long hard look at how we *do* Christmas while hoofing it on this Trek to the Manger. I've had people tell me they're taking it easy this year – easy on their expectations. Easy on their pocketbooks.

In light of the *real* gift of this season, some of us are choosing to deemphasize the gifts that distract our loved ones from *the* Gift the shepherds found in the manger on that holy night.

There's nothing like God's gift of Jesus to communicate His great love to all of us!

What message is *your* gift-giving going to send when Christmas morning rolls around?

My husband and I were watching an old episode of the TV series *Bones* – a Christmas episode. While expressing her distaste for gift-giving, Dr. Temperance Brennan pointed out that gifts aren't really given with the recipient in mind. Her scripted take on Christmas was that people give gifts that will make themselves look good to those who receive them. Christmas, she complained, is an entire "season dedicated to self-promotion."⁶

I had never thought about gift-giving in those terms before. Ouch! Because she's right (or at least on the right track).

Thinking back over today's shopping frenzy, replaying my thought track while deciding between this gift and that, I honestly was not thinking only about the one on the receiving end of my package. Many of my thoughts were about *me*.

That will never work! I don't want her to think I

really think that's her size.
I want him to think I know what's cool for guys his age. I want this gift to make an impression.
I don't want to seem cheap. Or old. Or out of touch. Or showy.

Maybe my gift-giving really is all about me.

Daily Giveaway

The burning question I'm left with makes me appropriately uncomfortable as I gather up the gift wrap, scissors and tape:

Who (or maybe, what) am I promoting with the packages I'm preparing to give away?

My ability to choose great gifts?
My financial situation?
My need for approval?
My need for attention (which I'll get, by the way, if you really like my gift)?
My thoughtfulness?
My feelings for you, my recipient?

In the gift of His Son for the salvation of humankind, God was promoting His love, His mercy and His plan. He even continues giving gifts to His children - things like love, joy, and peace. Gifts of abilities and talents. Gifts that benefit the world in need around us.

Maybe our gift-giving should look more like *that*.

I know you're probably more efficient than I am, and your packages are most likely already wrapped and in the mail. But what about the most important gift you can give this Christmas – the gift you give *to* the Baby in the manger when December 25 arrives?

The Wise Men's gifts were practical, useful, and valuable, yet what can we possibly lay at His feet that He doesn't already have? All that we have and everything that we are is ours because He gave it to us.

It's kind of like the way a child feels at Christmas time, wanting desperately to give Mom a good gift, but having to ask for her help (an idea, some money, and a ride to the mall) in order to give it.

I don't know about you, but I don't want to arrive empty-handed when our Trek to the Manger is complete.

When I finally reach His presence, I want to be able to offer the most practical, useful, and valuable gift to my Savior that I am capable of giving. But to have such a Giveaway means that I must first *receive* the gifts He has already given to me – forgiveness for my mistakes and shortcomings, life that will not end when my body's time is up, and the unbelievable riches infused into my life by His very real presence within.

To lay the perfect gift at the manger is going to require me to ask for His help, His ideas, His resources, and His time.

Let's get it done! Today is Gift Selection Day.

22 *TOUR GUIDES*

A couple of Octobers ago, my family took a whirlwind bus tour through the Washington, D.C. area. We boarded the bus in Virginia – early in the morning – and drove until we met up with the man who would be our tour guide. For the few hours before our guide joined us, we were subject to the driver's bad jokes, inappropriate commentary, and thinking-out-loud with the microphone on. We were all *so ready* for a change by the time our guide stepped onto the bus!

The tour guide had a voice that was easy to listen to. He had a plethora of information and knew how to tell a story. He was easy going and was able to make the historical sites come to life for our group.

We returned to Virginia that night feeling as if we had seen and learned and experienced everything we had hoped for, and then some.

Thanks to a wonderful tour guide.

Star Sighting
Part of being on this Trek to the Manger is realizing we're not on the path alone.

There are others walking alongside us. There are some who walk faster and some who lag behind, but our faith-walk itself is not solitary - it is done in the company of others.

Now, some of these *others* have an understanding of God that is similar to our own. These are the people who sit beside us in the pew on Sunday mornings, or who study the Scriptures with us during the week. All of us know at least a few like-minded believers whose trek is remarkably parallel to ours. It's easy to walk with these trekkers. We understand them, and we see the path much in the same way they do.

But what about those whose walk is very different from ours? What about those whose feet may not even be completely on the path?

What is our role, as followers of Jesus, in the lives of those who aren't like-minded, who don't see life and faith the way we do?

Author/speaker Rob Bell suggests we take a good long look at what it means to live as citizens of the Kingdom of God. Rather than seeing our job description as that of *missionary* – taking Jesus into the world – Bell cites the life of the Apostle Paul to make a case for *spiritual* tour guides:

"It is as if Paul is a spiritual tour guide and is taking

his readers through their world, pointing out the true and the good wherever he sees it… teaching people to use their eyes to see things that have always been there; they just didn't realize it. You see God where others don't. And then you point him out."[7]

As followers of the Light of the World, it's time we adopt a new understanding of what it means to walk in faith. We can keep to ourselves and hide inside the bubble of Christendom, absorbed in the trappings of our own little world, or we can look with wide-eyed wonder at all that we encounter, watching with eyes of faith and pointing out the good stuff of God when we see it.

Kind of like a well-trained tour guide, whose manner is easy going, whose stories are riveting, and who can make the confusing world around us spring into focus.

Daily Giveaway
I recently re-Tweeted an insightful comment related to how we shine our light in the world. Remember the bus driver on my D.C. tour? He was over the top when it came to noise, commentary, and inconsequential information. Sometimes we Christians resemble the bus driver more than the tour guide.

We do this when we assume that people need to hear *what* we have to say *when* we are ready to say it.

We do this when we forge ahead, ignoring the signals of those who just aren't interested in our commentary.

We do this when we don't let others get a word in edgewise, unapologetically monopolizing every conversation.

If we do these things, thinking we are shining God's light into the world, we are in desperate need of this simple advice:

"You can still be the light without having your high beams on and annoying everybody."
(Bob Goff, Twitter)

Look around you today, on this shared Trek to the Manger.

Who is traveling with you; keeping pace, keeping step?

Who has fallen behind and could use your encouragement and insight?

Who is peripheral to the path – or, as my friend Clareen said, who in your life is like a ship without a captain? What can you see through your eyes of faith that they may be missing and need desperately to see?

As Trekkies – followers of Jesus on a Trek to the Manger – our job description most closely matches that of a tour guide.

When we shine the light of Christ in the world, people will be *drawn* and people will be *listening*. Like the captive audience on a moving tour bus, each one of us has influence that impacts the lives of others.

Let's resolve today to be effective tour guides of the Kingdom, sending happy tourists home feeling as if they have seen, learned, and experienced everything they had hoped for.

And then some.

[7] P. 87-88 ROB BELL, *"VELVET ELVIS: REPAINTING THE CHRISTIAN FAITH"*
© 2005 BY ROB BELL, PUBLISHED BY ZONDERVAN

23 *TURN! TURN! TURN!*

We've all heard stories – some of us have lived them – about road trips gone awry due to a failure to *turn*. My family has such a story, when we missed our turn in the Rocky Mountains and wound up 30 miles down the wrong road before our error was discovered.

Annoyed and frustrated by the time we'd lost, we had no choice but to turn around and retrace our snow packed tire tracks back to the highway that would ultimately bring us home.

Turning is inevitable on the road. Without purposeful turns along the way, we may never reach our destination – be it the grocery store, the library, or Grandma's house.

Pete Seeger knew what he was talking about when he put the words of Ecclesiastes chapter 3 to music in the song, *"Turn! Turn! Turn! (To Everything There is a Season)."* You're probably hearing the tune in your head even now, with the harmonies of The Byrds bouncing from one neural transmitter to another:

To everything (Turn! Turn! Turn!)
There is a season (Turn! Turn! Turn!)
And a time to every purpose under Heaven.[8]

King Solomon's experimental life resulted in some pretty heavy conclusions, which you'll find summarized in the pages of Ecclesiastes. Solomon concludes that there is a time for everything – life, death, love, war, peace, silence, speech... All of which makes perfect sense in light of the world we live in.

The thing that captures my attention today, though, is the part Pete Seeger added to King Solomon's words. The part that says:
"Turn! Turn! Turn!"

Star Sighting

Our Trek to the Manger has undoubtedly not been perfectly straight, or perfectly smooth. No matter how hard we try, our human efforts always seem to land us 30 miles past our exit, requiring a strategic U-turn.

You may have made every attempt to follow the star – the Light of God's presence among us – throughout this season of Advent. Your best intentions may have been to give away the stuff of this world so you could simply focus on giving away the *good* stuff – love and acceptance of others as God's Son Himself has taught us to do.

It never fails, my friends. We miss the mark. We miss the road. And we have to *turn, turn, turn.*

The word *repent* is, in my simple understanding, equivalent to the words *turn, turn, turn.* Hear it this way, through the prophet Ezekiel's words to God's people:

"Therefore, O house of Israel, I will judge you, each one according to his ways, declares the Sovereign Lord. Repent! Turn away from all your offenses; then sin will not be your downfall. Rid yourselves of all the offenses you have committed, and get a new heart and a new spirit. Why will you die, O house of Israel? For I take no pleasure in the death of anyone, declares the Sovereign Lord. Repent and live!"
Ezekiel 18:30-32 *(NIV)*

To repent is to TURN – *away from our sin, away from our idols, away from our small and self-focused existence.*

To repent is to TURN – *toward the light of God's grace, and His mercies that continue to be new for us each and every day.*

To repent is to change our minds, to veer off the ill-navigated path, and to choose a new direction as illuminated by the light of our Father's presence.

To repent is to make a U-turn – *do a 180* – leaving

the old road behind and making a Trek to the Manger.

To repent is to *turn, turn, turn*.

Daily Giveaway
Sometimes we try to fix our mistakes and cover our sins with a series of small adjustments. We might tweak our behavior and justify the subtle change with words like these:

It's easier to change a little at a time.
Going cold turkey hurts.
God knows how hard it is to change a life-long habit/relationship/behavior like mine.

The problem is, our small changes in attitude and changes in latitude don't always add up to a *turn*.

The God who inspired Ezekiel, King Solomon, and Pete Seeger is waiting right here, right now, for you and me to take Him at His Word. He has promised all things are possible for the one who believes in His Son (Mark 9:23), and that includes making the U-turn your life in Christ requires today.

It's one thing to be on a road trip gone wrong because of a failure to turn, but it's quite another to travel through a life gone wrong because we were too distracted, too disoriented, or too darn stubborn to *turn, turn, turn.*

What are you waiting for? *It's your turn.*

[8] WRITTEN BY PETE SEEGER/BOOK OF ECCLESIASTES, *"TURN! TURN! TURN! (TO EVERYTHING THERE IS A SEASON)"* WAS RELEASED ON THE BYRDS' ALBUM *"TURN! TURN! TURN!"* IN 1965 ©COLUMBIA RECORDS

24 STINKY FRIDAY

Like it or not, when my alarm goes off each Friday morning, it has officially begun...

Stinky Friday.

New to our family traditions, Stinky Friday was instituted through the back door by my sixth grade son shortly after school began. If you're a parent, you may have noticed how much harder it is to rouse your sleeping students by the time Friday morning rolls around. It took about three weeks of middle school before the Friday phenomenon showed up on my radar, and I realized that no alarm clock seemed to be able to cut through the Friday morning fog.

I'm a slow learner, but one lesson God has graciously allowed me to repeat many times is the one that teaches *choose your battles*. I decided that making my son get up in time for a shower on Friday mornings was not a battle worth choosing, so I unofficially let it slide (to my son's great joy). Upon hearing about this decision I had made, my husband coined the consequences *Stinky Friday*.

Star Sighting

Ever been camping? By day three things can get pretty stinky.

Been on a plane lately? Not everyone who buys a ticket boards the plane smelling shower fresh.

After days and days on the road, I imagine things might have gotten pretty ripe for the Wise Men (they were traveling with camels, after all).

A byproduct of travel is perspiration.
A byproduct of perspiration is odor.

It simply goes with the territory.

The act of living produces a similar byproduct, according to the prophet Isaiah. Just like body odor, to which none of us is immune (to which your medicine cabinet will attest), our words and actions contribute to what ends up being the *Ground Hog Day* of Stinky Fridays:

"All of us are dirty with sin. All the right things we have done are like filthy pieces of cloth."
Isaiah 64:6a *(NCV)*

Even our best efforts at living produce the inevitable byproduct of stinky sin.

It simply goes with the territory.

The best remedy for body odor is a long shower and the help of some powerful (lightly scented) toiletries.

And the best remedy for sin-stained lives is the water of baptism, through which pours the powerful Spirit of God:

"It wasn't so long ago that we ourselves were stupid and stubborn, dupes of sin, ordered every which way by our glands, going around with a chip on our shoulder, hated and hating back. But when God, our kind and loving Savior God, stepped in, he saved us from all that. It was all his doing; we had nothing to do with it. He gave us a good bath, and we came out of it new people, washed inside and out by the Holy Spirit. Our Savior Jesus poured out new life so generously. God's gift has restored our relationship with him and given us back our lives."
Titus 3:3-7 *(The Message)*

God's gift to Trek-weary travelers is a good bath in His sea of forgetfulness.

Now that's a star that I can follow.

Daily Giveaway
Perhaps the best thing you can give away on Stinky Friday - and every day - is the understanding that *all* of us are dirty with sin.

We can be the most diligent followers of Christ,

the most purposefully generous of people, yet on our best day we look no better than mud-stained, grass-stained jeans. Our only hope for emerging from this life in the pristine white robes of the saints is to be washed in the saving blood of the *once child, now sacrificial Lamb of God*, whose cleansing is offered without qualification to all who have breath. No exceptions.

The life-giving work of the cross is *God's work*, not ours.

On this Stinky Friday, let's choose to embrace the level playing field of souls that are the men, women, and kids we encounter every day.

In light of the good bath you've been given, find a way today to share the sweet fragrance of restoration with someone whose own stain removal efforts have failed over and over again.

By giving us back our lives, God makes it possible for us to reach out and guide others onto the path – this *lifelong* Trek to the Manger.

25 *I CALL SHOTGUN!*

Do you remember what it was like to be 15 years old – almost old enough to drive? You may have had your driver's permit, but you could just about taste your need to sit behind the wheel of a car and just... *drive*. Without Mom or Dad in the passenger seat.

Oh, the freedom!
Oh, the independence!
Oh, the control!

I've logged a whole lot of hours behind the wheel since the Sweet 16. Driving kids to school. Driving scouts to camp. Driving to visit my family, across the state or across the country. I've put hundreds of thousands of miles on vehicles while motoring down many, many roads.

Funny, but time seems to have eliminated my craving to be the one to drive.

These days, I call Shotgun!

Star Sighting
Being a passenger is tough for some of us who struggle with control issues. I know all about

this, firsthand. To put your life into the hands of another driver raises the stress level and thickens the tension you feel about the journey.

What if he's not a safe driver?
What if we get in an accident?
What if a tire blows and she doesn't know what to do?
What if he dozes off when he gets tired?
What if she doesn't know how to drive on ice?
What if... fill in the blank?

These feelings are stronger and questions more unsettling when we don't know (or trust) the driver. Thoughts like these drifted through my mind while sitting beside my 15 year-old daughter in her first months behind the wheel. Many, *many* times I fought the urge to have her pull over and switch seats with me. I wasn't a good passenger and I knew it (she knew it, too, and won't hesitate to tell you so).

One day Jesus found Himself in a similar situation with His followers. They were questioning Him and His teachings, doubting and stressing out. They *said* they would follow Him, but their words and actions sent a very mixed message. Jesus had some difficult words for them that day:

"Anyone who intends to come with me has to let me lead. You're not in the driver's seat; I am. Don't run from suffering; embrace it. Follow me and I'll show

you how. Self-help is no help at all. Self-sacrifice is the way, my way, to saving yourself, your true self. What good would it do to get everything you want and lose you, the real you?"
Mark 8:34-36 *(The Message)*

Correct me if I'm wrong, but wasn't Jesus saying that the only way you're getting into *this* car is by giving up the driver's seat and calling *Shotgun*?

Choosing to be seated in second place?

Allowing Him to take you where it is that He intends to go?

Daily Giveaway
How we give up the steering wheel of our lives matters to God.

Do we do so *reluctantly*, climbing into the passenger seat with a pout, arms crossed and teeth clenched?

Do we *seem* to be willing to let Him drive, yet continually reach over and try to grab the wheel from Him, relinquishing control when the going gets rough?

Or do we, like an enthusiastic passenger (think of the 12 year old in your life), cry out *Shotgun!* while in a dead run for the passenger side door?

The only way we will easily give up the driver's seat of our earthly cars is by trusting the driver to do the right thing. To make the right turns. To pay attention to the hazards on the road. When we trust like *that*, being a passenger is easy.

Riding Shotgun is the best seat in the car!

The only way we can easily give up the driver's seat of our complicated lives is by trusting the Driver to do the right thing. To make the right turns. To pay attention to the hazards on the trek ahead. When we trust like *that*, being a follower of Jesus is easy.

Riding Shotgun is absolutely the best seat in *that* car!

As our Trek to the Manger approaches an end, we're going to have to give away some *trust*. It's time we take Jesus seriously and stop fighting for the driver's seat in our own lives. It's time we ask ourselves whether we really believe that Jesus intends to lead us, to care for us, and to show us a better way of living.

Do you trust Him? Really? Enough to give your control and your car keys away?

What lies ahead is the adventure of a lifetime.

I call Shotgun!

ROAD CLOSED

If you've ever traveled in the northern states during winter months, you know about road closures. Some of the most brutal winter storms I've ever had the misfortune to experience took place while living in Wyoming. There are actually permanent *Road Closed* signs, mounted on moveable gates, throughout the state. These gates are lowered to block the driving lanes of roads and highways when the blowing snow and ice make driving impossible.

If you're lucky, you'll be at home when stormy weather hits. If you're not, well, you probably have a story like this one.

One winter, before my husband and I were married, my family decided to fly to Mexico for Christmas. We nearly got stuck in Denver while blizzard snows swirled around our plane and the pink de-icing fluid dripped down the window glass. At one point as we moved toward the runway, finally cleared for take-off, the entire assembly of beach-bound passengers broke into a chorus of this familiar Christmas song:

Oh, the weather outside is frightful
But the beach will be delightful
So as long as there's Mexico
Let it snow! Let it snow! Let it snow!

It was a perfectly wonderful, warm Christmas that year. For me.

Not so for my husband-to-be.

Shortly after I arrived in paradise, Dallas set out on the Wyoming roads. He was miles and miles from his destination when the Highway Patrol began diverting traffic into a very (did I say *very*?) small town, because the road had been closed. Hundreds of holiday travelers were herded into the town's community center, because there was seriously *no room at the inn.*

Families with children, seniors traveling with pets, and people from all walks of life converged on the small town of Chugwater, Wyoming. No alternatives. No way out.

Road Closed.

Star Sighting
Of course it was a *long* 24 hours before the road re-opened and my fiancé and his many temporary roommates could move on.

Some people didn't handle the wait very well.

Some yelled too much. Some drank too much.
Some chose to shiver in their cars rather than keep
warm in the crowded gymnasium all night.

For some, the closed road brought out the very
worst in behaviors and attitudes. But there were
exceptions.

The town of Chugwater is known (albeit in small
circles) for its chili. Residents on that night got
together and made batches and batches of their
chili to share with the hungry travelers. People
brought board games and card games to distract
the stranded travelers. Someone brought in
videos for the children to watch. A great effort
was made by a few generous hearts to make the
road closure less burdensome for those who
were anxious to move on.

Some of the travelers appreciated the gestures of
hospitality. Some of them said "thank you."
Some played the games and actually had a pretty good
time. Some made the best of an inconvenient situation
and let the light inside of them shine through.

Happily, I was on the beach through all of this,
but I can't help but wonder just what I would
have done.

The prophet Isaiah says:

"The Holy can be either a Hiding Place or a Boulder

blocking your way."
Isaiah 8:14 *(The Message)*

Like those who reached the sign that said *"Road Closed"* and chose to make the best of it, we can choose to seek refuge in the Holy when our best-laid plans are undone.

Or, like those whose bitterness over a situation they could not control bred anger and discontent, we can see God's plans and His presence as a great big boulder standing between where we are today and where we want to be tomorrow.

And we can let it eat at us and make us less than we were intended to be.

Daily Giveaway
On our Trek to the Manger, and in our faith walk through life, we are going to come across roads that God has closed. It's possible He's closed them to keep us safe – to protect us from the elements, risks, and hazards that lie ahead. Inevitably, some of those road closures are going to catch us off guard and require that we rethink our travel plans.

With this in mind, let's shift focus to those in our lives who are in such a place today. How can we, like the residents of Chugwater, extend the hand of friendship and care to those who are stranded on the road around us?

Can we make them a meal?
Can we help divert their attention and bring a smile,
if only for a couple of hours?
Can we share our warmth and comfort while they
rest?
Can we possibly shed some light into their darkness,
or suggest a safe detour to get them back on the road?

Today, let's give away some *chili* and some *hope* that the road will reopen and the journey will end exactly how the Holy had it planned all along.

Let it snow! Let it snow! Let it snow!

27 *ARE WE THERE YET?*

You've heard it before. You may have heard it this week! It's the mantra of weary travelers world-wide:

Are we there yet?

Not specifically reserved for kids, this question has probably littered every backseat of every car in every country during road trips of every kind.

It tells us you're *tired*.
It tells us you're *bored*.
It tells us you're *anxious*.
It tells us you're *ready to arrive*.

Our Trek to the Manger has been a long one (and it isn't over yet!). Some of us have focused diligently on the challenges of the path, and what has resulted is a very different season of Advent than any we've traveled before.

But some of us are just ready to be there already! To be *present* with the Christ child. To have *arrived* at our heart's seasonal destination – the point where God became human and began to teach us how to live as Kingdom subjects in this temporary world. Some of us today can't keep our road-weary selves from asking the age-old question:

Are we there yet?

Star Sighting
In his prophecies regarding the coming Messiah, Isaiah writes of the promises of God concerning the future:

"I'll install Peace to run your country, make Righteousness your boss. There'll be no more stories of crime in your land, no more robberies, no more vandalism. You'll name your main street Salvation Way, and install Praise Park at the center of town. You'll have no more need of the sun by day nor the brightness of the moon at night. God will be your eternal light, your God will bathe you in splendor. Your sun will never go down, your moon will never fade. I will be your eternal light. Your days of grieving are over. All your people will live right and well, in permanent possession of the land... I am God. At the right time I'll make it happen."
Isaiah 60:17b-22 (The Message)

For those of us whose hearts are longing to arrive at *this* place – this place of eternal light in the presence of God – celebrating yet another Christmas season can seem almost tedious.

And that's okay.

If deep inside your heart is crying *Are we there yet?* you are in good company.

These mileposts we reach along the way, celebrations like Christmas and Easter, are part of the fabric of the one-of-a-kind life God is weaving for you and for me. But something inside us knows that when we reach the Manger this week, we will not have finally *arrived*.

It's just another milepost, and in a few days we will move on.

Even with all of the joy and excitement of Christmas, we will find ourselves on December 26 asking the same old, tired question of our patient, tireless God:

Are we there yet?

Daily Giveaway
Soon we, like the Wise Men, will arrive at a new understanding of the Holy in light of the brokenness we see and feel.

Soon we, like the shepherds, will worship a God who took the form of a baby so we might grow up in relationship with Him.

Soon we will arrive at the big day! How are you feeling? *Excited? Anxious? Nervous? Stressed out? Apathetic? Indifferent? Bored?*

My heartfelt prayer – for all of us Trekkies – is that we would find ourselves experiencing Christ's birth in unexpected and surprising ways.

Some of us have arrived at many Christmases in our lifetimes. Don't allow your autopilot to engage, stealing the joy from the most important message we will ever hear – that God is with us.

He is here!

Today, consider the possibility that we've been asking the wrong question all along. Instead of asking *Are we there yet?* perhaps the better question is: *Do I believe that God is here?*

If you believe Emmanuel has come, consider what might happen when you give away the temptation to look forward to the future at the expense of here and now.

Don't worry about tomorrow.

Be present today with our ever-present God!

28 *AGLOW*

When I lived in southwestern Arizona, to travel anywhere required hours of trekking through the desert. I remember many times returning from the east where, save for the lights of a few very small towns, once the night settled in, darkness fell.

I always knew we were getting close to home on those dark nights when the lights of San Luis, Mexico appeared on the southern horizon, setting the sky above the city aglow; giving testimony to the energy and activity of a city that I, to this day, have never actually seen.

Sometimes, when conditions were right, the sky seemed to soak up the city lights, emitting an almost eerie glow into the otherwise black blanket of sky. On nights like these, you'd have thought it was New York City in the distance!

As the Wise Men approached Bethlehem, they too saw an energetic glow in the skies above the little town... only the Light *they* encountered had less to do with electricity and more to do with *epiphany*.

Star Sighting

At night, light is an indicator of energy and activity.

When you enter a room, you turn on the light.
Your Christmas lights twinkle best after dark.
And before you settle into bed, after putting down
your book, one of the last things you do is turn out
the light.

In the darkness, when a light is on, someone is usually awake and active, using energy.

And when it's *really* dark, people are drawn to that light.

The star that the Wise Men saw above Bethlehem was an indicator of energy and activity, too. God had entered our darkness, and He was preparing to turn on the Light of the World! His Light would make it possible for us to see well enough to read the writing on the wall (and the writing in the Word).

His Light would draw us toward Him, capturing our attention (and our imagination).

Unlike our necessary bedtime rituals, the Light born into the world that night will never go out. As the Wise Men approached their well-lit destination, the energy and activity of *this* Light was just getting started!

It is this same Light that draws us still.

Daily Giveaway

You may have noticed that the world we live in is growing increasingly dark. Sorrow and hopelessness are well-stocked on the shelves of the stores we're shopping in, my friends. People you know have a cart-full already and are waiting in line to check out.

This pervasive darkness ought to make the Light of the Christ child blazingly obvious! Why, then, do we feel as if our own Light-filled lives look more like dying embers than the powerful beam of a searchlight at night?

I think it's because we're trying to shine God's Light *alone*.

You don't get a glow like San Luis in the desert by shining your solitary light into the night. Only when you join with others whose energy comes from the Light and whose activity reflects His heart can you ever hope to fill the sky with the proof of His presence!

Jesus said it like this:

"You're here to be light, bringing out the God-colors in the world. God is not a secret to be kept.
We're going public with this, as public as a city on a hill." Matthew 5:14 *(The Message)*

Often Jesus' words are heard as if they were written just for *me*, but Jesus wasn't speaking to just one person. This was His famous Sermon on the Mount, and *many* people were present that day! Jesus knew that to set the world aglow, His followers would have to be united. A city! A city on a hill, whose community of lights would have the best possible chance of attracting the attention of those who live in darkness.

We often think of there being safety in numbers, but I propose that Jesus knew there would be *energy* in numbers, too! Today, take some time to consider the Christian community you call home.

What is the *source* of your community's energy? What does your community have energy *for*? How is this energy-in-action *displayed* in their homes, neighborhoods, workplaces, and cities?

Are you a part of the city on a hill that Jesus talked about, where none are hiding their Lights, but instead they are pooling their resources to set the sky aglow with the Light of the World?

If your community sets the darkness ablaze, take time to give away some appreciation to those who inspire and support you on your faith journey!

Maybe this means giving a special donation in honor

or support of this community of yours.

Maybe you need to write some thank you notes or make a phone call to let words of appreciation be heard.

Maybe you know of someone in your faith-city who is in need of help this Christmas? Slip a gift card in the mail or invite their family over for Christmas dinner.

Give your Light a chance to shine while stoking the flame in those you are traveling with!

If your community doesn't look much different than the darkness in these difficult times, maybe it's time to take a road trip.

Where do you see Light shining?

Is there a faith community whose energy and activity resonate with the way God has shaped you for service?

Don't let yourself get stuck thinking you're supposed to bloom where you're planted if where you're planted is not good soil.

Christian community that works the way God intended will illuminate the sky above and the world around them, making it pretty obvious where they are.

May you find, as we reach our destination, that

the star is but a *hint* of what's going on below! The real work is actually occurring in the startled cries of new life, exploding onto the scene one human being at a time.

Giving testimony to the energy and activity of a God who plans to light up the world through His people.

29 UNVEILED (DRIVING WITH THE TOP DOWN)

When we set out on this Trek to the Manger, the season of Advent was a blank slate – unwritten, with oodles of raw potential on the horizon. Like the Wise Men of old, we began a journey of unknowns, guided by a Light unlike any we had ever seen before.

I have stories to tell – I wonder if you do, too? – from this Advent adventure of ours! But before we begin to reminisce, we really must first *arrive*.

Star Sighting

Our approach may be tentative and uncertain, or maybe we're just so excited to see what God has in store that we cannot hold it in! Peeking around the corner or bursting through the door, our hungry eyes and hearts long to feast on our first glimpse of the Savior.

I believe God has something like *this* in mind for us, as we approach the Holy mystery of the manger:

"[*He will*] *throw wide the gates so good and true*

people can enter. People with their minds set on you,
you keep completely whole. Steady on their feet,
because they keep at it and don't quit."
Isaiah 26:2-3 *(The Message)*

And you have kept at it, my friend!
You have set your mind on the manger.
You have kept your eye on the Light.
You did not quit.

And tomorrow, as we arrive at our Advent destination, the God who brought you here will meet you here in Word and wisdom gained on the journey.

Moses met with God in person a long, long time ago. Scripture teaches that while in God's presence, Moses' face would radiate the reflected glory of God – to such a degree that he would wear a veil over his face when returning to the people. They wouldn't be able to handle all that Light.

Once the Tent of Meeting (and later, the Temple) had been built, only the priests of Israel were allowed to enter the Holy of Holies – the place where the presence of God dwelled. A veil was erected between this holy, restricted space and the part of the worship center where the ordinary people would gather.

When God sent His Son to become one of us, the

unseen veil between heaven and earth was torn in two. The holy invasion of the nativity served to give humans access to the Father in a way we never had before. And when Jesus took His very last human breath on the cross, the veil in the temple itself was ripped from top to bottom, serving as an exclamation point on the word *Emmanuel* – God with us!

Through the child we seek in the manger, God has thrown wide the gates for good and true people to enter. No longer separated from Him, we come into His very presence with the promise of these words:

"Only Christ can get rid of the veil… Whenever, though, they turn to face God as Moses did, God removes the veil and there they are – face to face! They suddenly recognize that God is a living, personal presence, not a piece of chiseled stone. And when God is personally present, a living Spirit, that old, constricting legislation is recognized as obsolete. We're free of it! All of us! Nothing between us and God, our faces shining with the brightness of his face. And so we are transfigured much like the Messiah, our lives gradually becoming brighter and more beautiful as God enters our lives and we become like him."
2 Corinthians 3:14b-18 *(The Message)*

Nothing between us!
Our faces shining with the brightness of Him!
Can you feel it?

It's kind of like driving a convertible with the top down.

Daily Giveaway

The best thing you can give away on this final day of our shared Trek to the Manger is the *lie* that you cannot change.

By spending time in the very real presence of the Spirit of God, we *are* changing! Gradually, you and I become brighter and more beautiful as God enters our lives and we begin to look like Him.

But for change to continue, we have to stop hiding behind homemade veils. We have to stop forcing our private agendas and personal preferences on the One in whose likeness we are being made.

We have to start driving with the top down.

Nothing between you, on the road, and the Light who guides you on your way. Hair tossed by gentle breezes. Fresh, invigorating air.

From this day on, it's you and God on a road revealed milepost by milepost - the adventure of a lifetime!

Merry Christmas, traveling buddy!

And Godspeed.

ACKNOWLEDGMENTS

This Trek to the Manger would be incomplete
without acknowledging my Traveling Buddies:

Dallas - *your love looks like Jesus to me*
Britton - *my daughter, my hero*
Joffrey - *filling our home with music and laughter
since 1998*

Mom & Dad - *my heart is safe with you*

Julie, Kimberly & Marlena - *your editorial honesty
is a rare spiritual gift*

February retreat girls - *it all began with you!*

ABOUT THE AUTHOR

Brita Hammit is on a journey, living into the unique identity and lively calling of God - *my Pink Shoes* - and inviting others to do the same.

Pink Shoes Ministries is on a mission, creating space for people of service and faith to breathe in the Holy against the backdrop of a broken world.

Visit Pink Shoes Ministries on the web for information about women's retreat events and curriculum:

pinkshoesministries.me

Made in the USA
San Bernardino, CA
05 December 2019

60945139R00080